CAVE GEOLOGISTS

Christine Honders

New York

Published in 2016 by The Rosen Publishing Group, Inc.
29 East 21st Street, New York, NY 10010

First Edition

Editor: Katie Kawa
Designer: Mickey Harmon

Photo Credits: Cover gremlin/E+/Getty Images; pp. 4–5, 18–19, 22–23 (main) salajean/Shutterstock.com; pp. 6–7 muratart/Shutterstock.com; p. 8 Bartlomiej K. Kwieciszewski/Shutterstock.com; p. 9 (cave bacon) https://commons.wikimedia.org/wiki/File:CaveBacon.jpg; p. 9 (cave column) IrinaK/Shutterstock.com; p. 9 (cave draperies) Doug Meek/Shutterstock.com; pp. 11–12 Evgeny Gorodetsky/Shutterstock.com; p. 12 https://wikimediafoundation.org/wiki/File:%C3%89douard-Alfred_Martel_(1895).jpg; p. 13 Westend61/Getty Images; pp. 14–15 Carsten Peter/Speleoresearch & Films/National Geographic/Getty Images; pp. 16–17 Dudarev Mikhail/Shutterstock.com; p. 21 Adam Jones/Science Source/Getty Images; p. 23 (inset) Matt Jeppson/Shutterstock.com; pp. 24–25 Ginger Livingston Sanders/Shutterstock.com; p. 27 Robbie Shone/Aurora/Getty Images; pp. 28–29 https://wikimediafoundation.org/wiki/File:Mammoth_Cave_tour.jpg; p. 30 David Herraez Calzada/Shutterstock.com.

Cataloging-in-Publication Data

Honders, Christine.
Cave geologists / by Christine Honders.
p. cm. — (Out of the lab: extreme jobs in science)
Includes index.
ISBN 978-1-5081-4513-4 (pbk.)
ISBN 978-1-5081-4514-1 (6-pack)
ISBN 978-1-5081-4515-8 (library binding)
1. Caves — Juvenile literature. 2. Geology — Vocational guidance — Juvenile literature. 3. Geologists — Juvenile literature. I. Honders, Christine. II. Title.
QE34.H66 2016
550.23—d23

Manufactured in the United States of America

CPSIA Compliance Information: Batch #BW16PK: For Further Information contact Rosen Publishing, New York, New York at 1-800-237-9932

Contents

COOL CAVE SCIENCE

When you think of a scientist, you probably think of someone in a laboratory, or lab, wearing a white coat and looking into a microscope. To some people, being a scientist doesn't sound like a very exciting job. Don't say that to Dr. Giovanni Badino! He doesn't spend much time in a lab. Most of his time is spent underground, studying caves.

The study of caves isn't attractive to many scientists. Caves have no natural light and many tight, enclosed spaces. However, there are certain scientists, such as Dr. Badino, who are willing to take on these challenges, no matter how **dangerous** they are. These scientists explore amazing, underground worlds that can't be seen on a map. Read on to find out more about the extreme scientists known as cave geologists, as well as other speleologists.

SCIENCE IN ACTION

Cave geologists study the rocks and minerals in caves to learn about the history of Earth. Speleology is a wider branch of science that deals with the general study of caves. Speleologists also study other parts of caves, such as underground water and cave-dwelling animals.

The word "speleology" comes
from the Greek word for "cave."

WHAT MAKES A CAVE?

Caves are natural openings in the ground large enough for people to walk through. They can be the size of a small room, or they can go on for miles with connecting passages. Some caves are formed by underground water that **dissolves** rocks along their natural cracks. Over thousands of years, this causes large chambers to form. Caves are also formed by lava from volcanoes, as well as by ocean waves.

Cave geologists study beautiful cave features called **speleothems**. Stalactites are speleothems formed by water dripping from a cave's ceiling. **Calcite** in the water is left behind over many years, creating formations that look like icicles hanging down. When drops of water hit a cave's floor, they create stalagmites, which look like icicles growing up from the ground.

Many cave geologists believe the colors of speleothems are determined by the minerals in the water. Calcite is white or colorless, but other minerals in the water combine with calcite to make colors.

STALACTITES

STALAGMITES

SCIENCE IN ACTION

There are about 17,000 known caves in the United States. However, new caves are still being discovered, so that number could increase at any time.

LEARNING FROM ROCKS

Stalagmites and stalactites aren't the only rock formations cave geologists study. Many different rock formations are found in caves, and each one tells geologists something different about the part of Earth they're studying.

Sometimes, stalagmites and stalactites grow together. They form a column, or a rock formation that goes from the floor of a cave to its ceiling. Another kind of rock formation in caves is called a drapery. Cave geologists believe draperies form when water runs down the walls of the cave. Draperies sometimes have stripes that make them look like bacon. Some geologists call these rock formations cave bacon! Geologists study the shape, size, and mineral composition of these rock formations to learn more about how caves are created.

CAVE POPCORN

SCIENCE IN ACTION

Cave popcorn is a rock formation that's often formed by water splashing in a cave and leaving calcite behind. The calcite forms small growths that look like the popcorn you get at a movie theater!

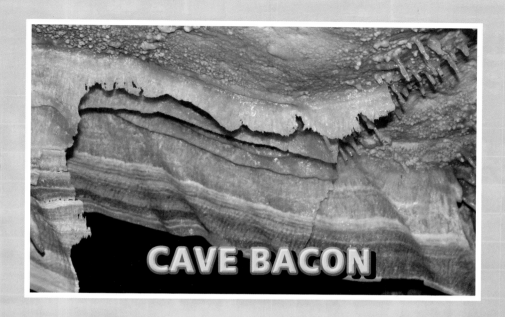

CAVE BACON

Cave geologists learn a lot about Earth's history from the many rock formations found inside caves.

CAVE COLUMN

CAVE DRAPERIES

A LOOK INTO THE PAST

Caves are beautiful to look at and interesting to explore. They also serve as underground labs for cave geologists and other scientists. Caves are rich in minerals for geologists to study. Fossils are also commonly found in caves. Geologists use fossils to learn what Earth was like millions of years ago.

The rock formations found in caves have been protected from outside forces, which gives scientists an **accurate** record of changes in climate, soil, plant life, and water in an area over thousands of years. This is useful for cave geologists who study climate change.

Early humans used caves for shelter and burying their dead. Some caves contain **artifacts** that help scientists called **archaeologists** learn more about early humans' lives.

SCIENCE IN ACTION

Water is one of the most important resources found in caves. Areas with many caves have some of the best wells in the world for producing water.

While geologists study the rock formations in caves, other speleologists study the water in caves.

THE FATHER OF SPELEOLOGY

Speleology is an interdisciplinary science. This means it involves many different areas of science, including geology, biology, and chemistry. Speleologists must also have a knack for drawing maps and **surveying** land. In the early days of speleology, these scientists had no formal training. They had to teach themselves about caves.

One early speleologist was Édouard-Alfred Martel, who was a Frenchman known to many as the father of speleology. He wasn't a trained scientist at all—he was actually a lawyer! However, by 1899, he was doing research in caves full time.

Martel would go down a deep, dark hole while hanging from a single rope. There was no equipment for cave exploration in the early 1900s, so he developed his own.

SCIENCE IN ACTION

Martel didn't just explore caves. He was the first person to map many caves throughout Europe.

Martel was the first to discover and map the hidden worlds of many caves, including the Gouffre de Padirac in France, which is shown here.

THE UNDERGROUND PHYSICIST

Martel paved the way for today's speleologists, including Dr. Giovanni Badino. When Dr. Badino was 17 years old, he went on a caving adventure and discovered he loved studying caves. He then went to college and got a degree in physics, which is the branch of science that deals with the interaction between matter and energy. Eventually, he combined his interest in caves with his science knowledge and became a speleologist.

Dr. Badino is an expert in speleogenesis, or the formation of caves, in glaciers. He also studies underground climates. Dr. Badino works out of the University of Turin in Italy, but his interest in caves has taken him all over the world. He's led teams of researchers to Brazil, Mexico, Pakistan, and Iceland. He's even traveled to Antarctica to study the ice caves there.

SCIENCE IN ACTION

When Dr. Badino isn't researching in caves, he's often working in the underground lab he created near the University of Turin.

Dr. Badino has led expeditions to study many caves around the world, including Mexico's Cave of Crystals, shown here.

CAVES AND CLIMATE

Dr. Lisa Baldini and her husband, Dr. James Baldini, are also underground scientists. They're mainly interested in studying stalagmites to uncover clues about climate patterns throughout Europe's history. They've traveled to caves in countries such as Germany and Poland to study the chemical composition of stalagmites using the latest technology. By figuring out the chemical composition of each layer, they can tell many things about the conditions that created the stalagmite, including how hard it was raining and the temperature of the water.

Jessica Oster is another scientist using speleothems to study Earth's climate. Oster and her team of researchers from around the United States and the United Kingdom have traveled as far as India to study the growth of stalagmites and how that growth relates to climate patterns.

SCIENCE IN ACTION

Many scientists who conduct research in caves are paleoclimatologists. A paleoclimatologist is a scientist who studies the climates of past ages in Earth's history.

Stalagmites offer many clues about Earth's past that geologists and other scientists are just now beginning to uncover.

JOBS FOR CAVE GEOLOGISTS

Many scientists who work in caves study the relationship between caves and climate. However, there are plenty of other career paths to follow if you want to study the science of caves. Cave geologists work for government agencies that help protect the environment and natural resources. The U.S. Geological Survey National Research Program needs scientists to study the path, amount, and quality of the groundwater that creates caves. Others who study caves focus on engineering. They determine if the ground above caves is stable enough for the construction of new buildings.

Cave geologists also work in tourism and land management. Millions of people visit caves in the United States every year. Scientists teach tourists about the wonders of these caves. They're also responsible for protecting the caves and their natural beauty.

SCIENCE IN ACTION

According to Dr. Badino, speleology is still a relatively small field, with only about 1,000 scientists currently researching in caves. However, that number will increase as the technology used to study caves continues to improve.

People who explore caves for fun are called cavers, or spelunkers. Many cave geologists developed an interest in caves as young spelunkers.

WHAT TO STUDY

If studying the hidden world of caves sounds like fun to you, it's important to work hard in school, especially in science classes. Most colleges don't have programs for speleology or cave geology. People studying to be cave geologists get a degree in geoscience, or Earth science, and concentrate on geology and geography. They must go to college for at least four years, and some states require geologists to get a license to work in their state.

It's also helpful for speleologists to take classes in biology, chemistry, **hydrology**, and **climatology**. Some speleologists are experts in cartography, which is the study of making maps. Still others are knowledgeable in land management and focus on caves in national parks that are open to visitors.

SCIENCE IN ACTION

Cave geologists and other speleologists should have a strong background in science, but they should also know a lot about math. Measurements are an important part of studying caves, and taking and comparing measurements calls for strong math skills.

Western Kentucky University offers courses in cave science that involve visits to Mammoth Cave National Park in Kentucky, shown here.

21

SPECIAL SKILLS

In addition to being great researchers, cave geologists and speleologists must have other skills and qualities to help them work well in these extreme places. One very important quality is good problem-solving skills. A cave geologist must be able to think and act quickly if there's an emergency during their time underground. They must also be physically fit to use the climbing equipment necessary for this job.

Cave geologists can't be afraid of enclosed or dark spaces. Imagine being in a dark place underground, down so far you can't see the opening of the cave. A situation like this could be very scary! It's absolutely necessary to have confidence in your abilities and in the people you're working with.

SCIENCE IN ACTION

Some people study caves because they want to see animals no one has ever seen. The creatures that live deep in caves are called troglobites, and scientists are still discovering new species in caves around the world.

Cave geologists and other underground scientists encounter animals few people ever see, including the cave salamander.

CAVE SALAMANDER

DANGERS OF CAVE GEOLOGY

In 1994, Dr. Badino led a small team on a research trip to a cave called Sima Aonda in the South American country of Venezuela. Unexpectedly, heavy flooding created a 984-foot (300 m) waterfall. The waterfall dragged Dr. Badino and his team to the bottom of the cave. This was 1,148 feet (350 m) deep! It took them 20 hours to get back to the top of the cave. Luckily, they all survived.

The dangers of cave geology are obvious. It's easy to become trapped or to fall and get hurt. Rescuing someone from a cave can take hours, because the cave entrance is often far from the injured person.

It's always best to explore caves with a group of experienced people, especially if you're a beginner.

Even experienced cave geologists have safety rules. Never enter caves alone, and always tell someone where you're going and when you're coming back. Also, don't depend on a single flashlight. Always carry more than one source of light.

TECHNOLOGY AND EQUIPMENT

To stay safe and comfortable in a cave, every cave geologist needs the basics: a helmet with a headlight on top, sturdy boots, gloves, and layers of clothing. Cave geologists also recommend having at least three sources of light. Other equipment depends on the cave. **Vertical caves** can have narrow drops of hundreds of feet, so a single rope and **pulley** system is used. Caves with lots of water may require underwater breathing equipment.

Using technology in caves for research poses a **unique** set of problems. There's little space for big, bulky equipment, and there's limited time to record data because of the working conditions.

Dr. Badino's biggest challenge is that his equipment isn't advanced enough to measure small changes in cave temperatures. He uses 10 to 20 thermometers and takes the average value to measure changes.

SCIENCE IN ACTION

Cave geologists and anyone else who wants to explore a cave should know as much as possible about the cave before going inside. That allows explorers to bring the right gear and be as prepared as possible for an emergency.

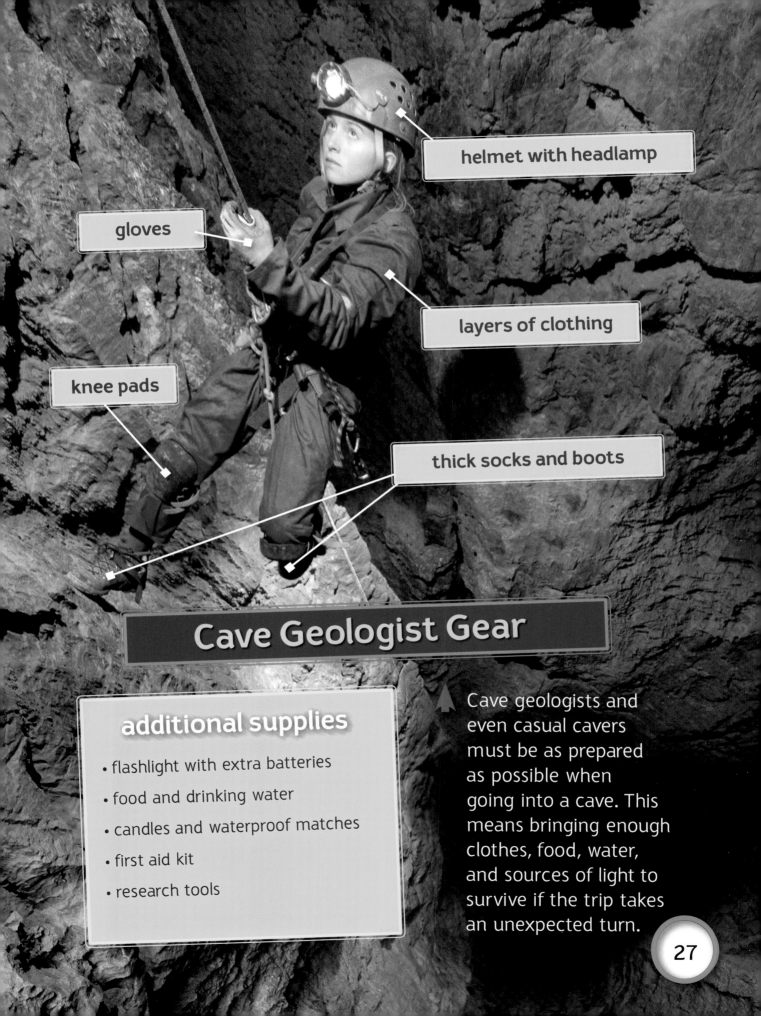

helmet with headlamp

gloves

layers of clothing

knee pads

thick socks and boots

Cave Geologist Gear

additional supplies

- flashlight with extra batteries
- food and drinking water
- candles and waterproof matches
- first aid kit
- research tools

Cave geologists and even casual cavers must be as prepared as possible when going into a cave. This means bringing enough clothes, food, water, and sources of light to survive if the trip takes an unexpected turn.

SEE FOR YOURSELF

Many cave geologists started out as spelunkers who explored caves for fun. Then, they decided they wanted to study the science of these fun and dangerous places. If you're interested in a career in caves, the first thing you should do is visit a cave to see these extreme places for yourself. It's important to always have an experienced adult with you when you go into a cave.

There are caves all over the United States for you to visit. Mammoth Cave is the world's longest cave system. It's over 400 miles (644 km) long. Some caves—including Mammoth Cave—even have a kids-only tour! Experienced rangers guide and teach young people all about this underground world.

SCIENCE IN ACTION

Stephen Bishop was an early explorer of Mammoth Cave. He was a slave who guided people on tours with an oil lamp. Bishop discovered parts of the cave you can still visit today.

A trip to a cave can give you a good sense of where you'd be working if you became a cave geologist.

EXTREME SCIENCE FOR EXTREME PEOPLE

It takes an extremely adventurous person to choose a career that involves studying science underground. Caves are beautiful places, but they can also be dangerous. These damp, dark, and sometimes very narrow places don't appeal to every scientist. However, to scientists who love caves, these underground worlds are the coolest places on Earth.

Cave geologists and other speleologists are pioneers, exploring places that have never been seen before and probably won't be seen by most people. They're finding new information about Earth's history and helping us better understand the planet we call home.

If you become a cave geologist, you could be the one leading your own team of scientists into these amazing underground worlds!

GLOSSARY

accurate: Free of mistakes.

archaeology: A science that deals with past human life through the study of material remains of people who lived long ago.

artifact: Something made by humans in the past.

calcite: A mineral composed of calcium and carbon that makes up limestone and chalk.

climatology: The scientific study of the weather in a certain place over a long period of time.

dangerous: Not safe.

dissolve: To break down a solid when a liquid mixes with that solid.

hydrology: The scientific study of water on, below, and above Earth's surface.

pulley: A wheel or set of wheels used with a rope or chain to lift or lower heavy objects.

speleothem: A structure formed in a cave by the dripping of mineral-rich water.

survey: To measure and examine an area of land.

unique: Special or different from anything else.

vertical cave: A long, narrow hole in the ground that goes straight down and is often called a pit.

INDEX

WEBSITES

Due to the changing nature of Internet links, PowerKids Press has developed an online list of websites related to the subject of this book. This site is updated regularly. Please use this link to access the list:
www.powerkidslinks.com/exsci/cvgeo